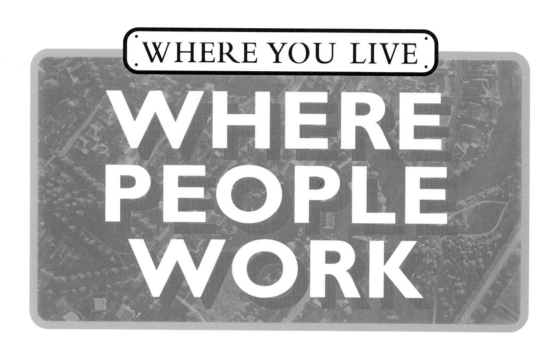

WHERE YOU LIVE

WHERE PEOPLE WORK

Ruth Nason

Photography by Chris Fairclough

FRANKLIN WATTS

LONDON•SYDNEY

First published in 2007 by
Franklin Watts
338 Euston Road
London NW1 3BH

Franklin Watts Australia
Level 17/207 Kent Street
Sydney NSW 2000

© 2007 Franklin Watts

ISBN: 978 0 7496 7173 0

Dewey classification number: 331.7

A CIP catalogue record for this book is available from the British Library.

Planning and production by Discovery Books Limited
Editor: Paul Humphrey
Designer: Ian Winton
Photography: Chris Fairclough

Printed in China

Franklin Watts is a division of Hachette Children's Books.

Photo acknowledgements
All the photographs in this book were supplied by Chris Fairclough except for those on pages 18 (top and bottom) Honda UK Manufacturing Ltd., 23 (bottom) Edison Mission Energy, 26 (top and bottom) Mary Evans Picture Library, 27 (top) The Potteries Museum and Art Gallery, Stoke-on-Trent.

Note about questions in this book
The books in the Where You Live series feature lots of questions for readers to answer. Many of these are open-ended questions to encourage discussion and many have no single answer. For this reason, no answers to questions are given in the books.

Contents

People at work

Everywhere you look there are people at work.

•What work do people do in an aeroplane?

•What people repair and look after buildings?

•Which people do you see at work in the street?

Work is very important. People work to earn money and pay for things that they and their family need.

•What work do people do in shops?
•Which people work to make the food that you and your family buy?

WHERE YOU LIVE
Ask the grown-ups in your family about the work that they do.

Work and home

This shopkeeper has his home above his shop. He lives and works in the same building.

LONDIS

CHURT NEWS & OR

opening hours

	am	pm
Monday	5.30 - 7.30	
Tuesday	5.30 - 7.30	
Wednesday	5.30 - 7.30	
Thursday	5.30 - 7.30	
Friday	5.30 - 7.30	
Saturday	5.30 - 7.30	
Sunday	5.30 - 1.30	

open

NO SMOKING

NO DOGS
Guide dogs excepted

- How many days each week does the shopkeeper work?
- What would it be like to live above a shop where your parents work?

play here.

DRY CLEANING + SHOE REPAIRS

Some people do their work in an **office** or a workshop that is a part of their home. A workshop is a place where people make things or mend things.

WHERE YOU LIVE
Find out if some children in your class have parents who work at home. What work do they do?

An artist's workshop is called a **studio**. This lady is a **sculptor**.

•What would be good about doing your work at home?

•What things do people need in an office?

•What things do we need people to mend for us?

•Why does a studio have a large window?

9

On the farm

Farmers live in houses on the land that they look after. Their work is all around them.

One type of building on the farm is a **barn**. Barns are used to store hay, to shelter animals and to keep machinery.

In parts of Britain where the **climate** is dry, more farmers grow **crops**.

•What crops do farmers grow in the part of Britain where you live?

•What work must farmers do to grow crops?

More farmers keep animals where the climate is wetter.

•Why do some farmers keep cows?

•What material do we get from sheep?

•Have you seen a barn that has been turned into a home?

WHERE YOU LIVE
See if you can visit a working farm or farm centre. Find one on the website listed in Further information on page 29.

Travelling to work

Most people travel from their home to their workplace. They make the journey often, so they want it to be easy.

Many people travel to work in a town or part of a city that is quite a long way from where they live. They are called **commuters**.

- How have these commuters travelled to work?
- Which other methods of transport do commuters use?
- When do most commuters travel?

WHERE YOU LIVE
Find out about your bus station or railway station. Where is it? What is it like? What work do the people do there?

Some people work as drivers. Their workplace moves!

Some lorry drivers go very long distances. Many drive to other countries.

In bad weather, driving for a living can be a dangerous job.

•What jobs can you think of that drivers do?
•How do lorries cross the sea to other countries?

Workplaces in towns

People work in shops, banks, libraries, cinemas, **restaurants** and petrol stations. All these places must be easy for **customers** to find and get to. Many are in the town centre.

- •Which types of workplaces can you see in these pictures?
- •What happens at a bank?
- •Where is a good place for a petrol station?

WHERE YOU LIVE
Do a survey of the types of workplaces in your main street. Are there offices above the shops?
Which people work in your main street in the evenings?

Some workplaces, such as **factories**, are built away from the town centre.

Factories, workshops, **warehouses**, offices and some shops may all be on a separate **industrial estate**.

•Why is it good for factories and industrial estates to be near a main road or a railway?

•Why is it good for workplaces to be in a separate estate, away from streets where people live?

People who help us

Every village, town and city needs people to:
- make decisions and organise things for the local people
- keep order
- help people who are ill
- rescue people in an emergency
- teach the children.

Find the workplaces of these people in the pictures on these two pages.

- Why does a fire station have a tower?
- What jobs do people do at your school?

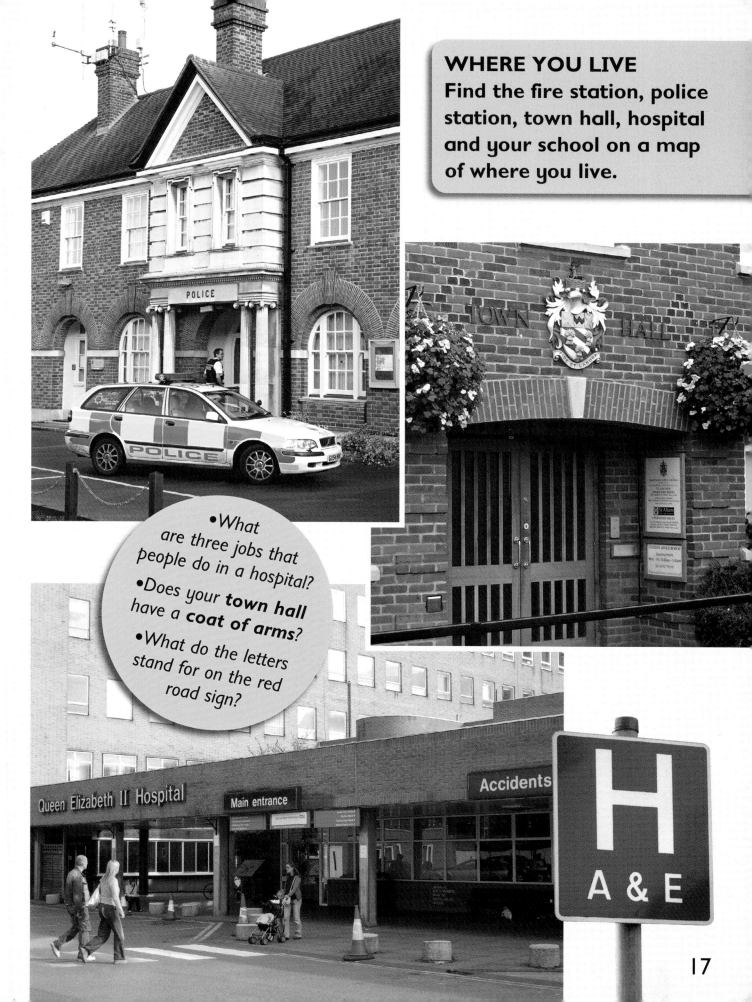

WHERE YOU LIVE
Find the fire station, police station, town hall, hospital and your school on a map of where you live.

POLICE

POLICE

TOWN HALL

- What are three jobs that people do in a hospital?
- Does your **town hall** have a **coat of arms**?
- What do the letters stand for on the red road sign?

Queen Elizabeth II Hospital   Main entrance

Accidents

H
A & E

Factories and warehouses

This **aerial view** shows the buildings and grounds of a car factory. It is on the edge of a town near a main road.

WHERE YOU LIVE
Find out how your village or town was affected when factories began to be built in Victorian times.

In a factory, machines are used to make large numbers of the same **goods**. The place where the goods are made is called the **production line**.

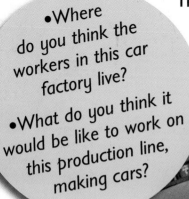

• Where do you think the workers in this car factory live?

• What do you think it would be like to work on this production line, making cars?

A warehouse is where goods are stored before they are sold. A **fork-lift truck** is used to lift heavy items on to high shelves.

Lorries go to and from factories and warehouses. Some bring **raw materials** to make the goods. Some take the finished goods away.

• Why do the rows of shelves in the warehouse have numbers on them?

• Why do you think the workers on this page wear yellow jackets like these?

• Can you think of other workers who wear jackets like this?

19

Offices

Offices can be just a small room for one or two people or a large space with many workers.

Office work includes:
- writing letters and emails
- making telephone calls
- holding meetings
- planning what needs to be done
- keeping records
- preparing **publicity**
- paying bills and sending bills
- keeping **accounts**.

•What jobs do you think are done in this office?

•How many computers can you see?

•What is your school office like?

Some offices are in buildings that used to be homes. Others are in specially built office blocks.

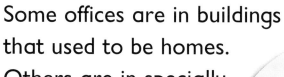

- Why are office buildings in a city built very high?

- Why do you think some houses are turned into offices?

WHERE YOU LIVE
Look for different styles of office buildings. Decide which you like best and least.

Working with Earth's resources

Farmers use the Earth's resources to give us food. Here are some more workers who supply things that we need from the Earth.

Forest workers grow trees and cut them down to produce wood. Some wood is used to make paper.

- What things do people make from wood?
- How is wood used to make paper?

Workers at a **quarry** take rock from the ground to use for building. Sometimes the rock is crushed and used in making roads.

Some people work to provide us with water. Water is collected in a **reservoir**. It is cleaned at a waterworks and travels through underground pipes to our homes.

- What is the difference between a quarry and a **mine**?
- How does water get into a reservoir?
- How is a reservoir shown on a map?

WHERE YOU LIVE
Visit a forest or a reservoir. What things can visitors do there?

By the sea

There are some jobs that people only do in places by the sea. For example, people work on fishing boats and **ferries** and at **ports**.

- Which is the nearest port to where you live?
- Where do the boats and ships go to?
- What work do people do at ports?

Think about what people do when they have a holiday by the sea. Then make a list of all the work that people do to help the holiday-makers have a good time.

- What workplaces are there in a holiday place by the sea?
- What happens to these workplaces in the winter?
- What are four types of work that people do in hotels?
- What does a lifeguard do?

WHERE YOU LIVE
Find hotels and other places where people work to help visitors to your town.

Changes at work

Work changes because people find new ways to do things.

One great change took place when people made machines and built the first factories. Before, most people worked on farms. They moved to work in the factories, and towns grew.

- How is this office worker from 130 years ago different from the modern workers on page 20?
- What does this photograph from 100 years ago tell you about the effect of the factories on towns?

Think how people's work changed after telephones, motor vehicles and computers were invented.

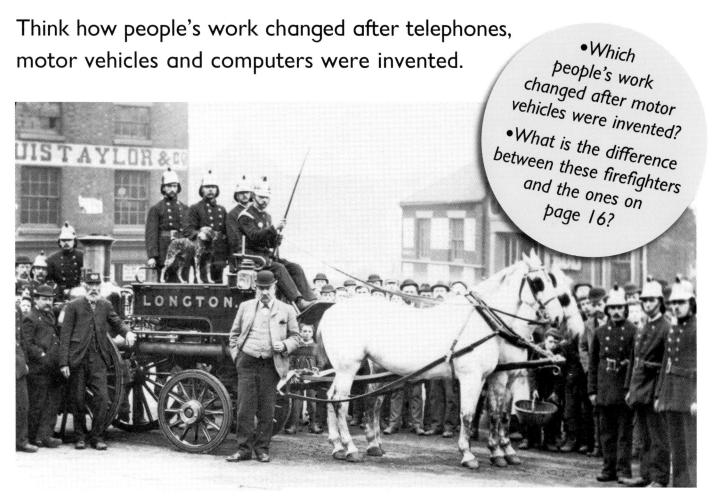

- Which people's work changed after motor vehicles were invented?
- What is the difference between these firefighters and the ones on page 16?

Where you live, look for old work buildings that have been changed into something else. For example, this old **mill** has been changed into offices for a newspaper.

WHERE YOU LIVE
Visit a local museum that tells you about the work that people did in the past.

- Do you know what a mill was used for?

Glossary

Accounts Records of money spent and money received, to show how much money is left.

Aerial view A view from the air, looking down on something.

Barn A building on a farm, like a large shed. It may be used to store crops, such as hay, to keep animals, such as cows, or as a place for farm machinery.

Climate The typical weather conditions of a region. It includes the average temperature and amount of rainfall, in different seasons.

Coat of arms A type of badge, for an organisation or a family, made from a group of symbols.

Commuters People who travel quite a long distance to their place of work every day, by train, bus or car.

Crops Plants, such as wheat and potatoes, that are grown and cared for until they are ripe and then gathered or picked, especially for use as food.

Customers The people who go to buy things that are for sale, and the people who go to be served in places such as restaurants and shoe menders.

Factories Buildings where goods are made.

Ferries Boats or ships that go to and fro across a stretch of water.

Fork-lift truck A truck with prongs, which the driver can raise or lower. It is used to lift objects onto and down from shelves.

Goods Items that are made for people to buy.

Industrial estate A separate area where all the buildings are workplaces, such as factories, warehouses, offices and some shops.

Mill A building where corn was ground to make flour.

Mine A place where workers dig useful materials, such as rock and coal, from deep under the ground.

Office A place where business is done. Office work includes writing, keeping records and organising things.

Ports Places on the coast where there is a harbour for boats and ships.

Production line A series or 'line' of jobs, done in a regular order, to make goods in a factory. A worker on a line always does the same job, at the same part of the line.

Publicity Advertisements, leaflets and other things that tell people about goods or services and try to persuade them to buy.

Quarry A place where workers dig useful rock from the surface of the ground.

Raw materials The materials that are used to make something.

Reservoir A lake made by people to store water.

Restaurants Places where meals are prepared and served to customers.

Sculptor An artist who carves stone or other materials to make statues, pictures and decorations on buildings.

Studio An artist's workroom. A studio also means a room for recording music, films, radio or TV programmes.

Town hall A building where work is done to organise the upkeep of a town. The mayor and councillors have meetings there.

Warehouses Buildings or rooms where goods are stored.

Further information

www.ukagriculture.com/
An easy-to-read website about agriculture and farming, with lots of pictures and some fun links.

www.forestry.gov.uk/learning
Here you can find pictures, videos, sound recordings and fact sheets about forests, including forestry work.

www.wessexwater.co.uk/kidzone/
index.aspx?id=337
Find out about the work that is done to bring us clean water.

www.virtualquarry.co.uk/
An interactive website about quarries, including a quarry tour.

Find out more about working farms and farm centres you can visit on:
britinfo.net/attractions/
attractions-L15000.htm

Books

Start-Up Geography: Jobs People Do (Evans Publishing)

When I'm at Work series (Franklin Watts) – includes books about a firefighter, a bus driver, a postman, a doctor and a recycling operative.

Out and About series (Franklin Watts) – includes books about the jobs people do in particular places from a fire station to a sports centre.

Just the Job series (Franklin Watts) – includes books in which young people talk about their work, for example, *I Work on a Building Site* and *I Work in a Supermarket*.

People Who Help Us series (Franklin Watts) – includes books about different types of workers, for example *At the Health Centre* or in *The Police*.

Visits

Some places of work in your town may arrange visits from school parties or hold 'open days' for people to find out what they do.

There may also be a local museum, where you can learn about ways of work and workplaces in the past.

Special places to visit include:
Cadbury World, near Birmingham, where you can make a tour of part of the chocolate factory. See
www.cadburyworld.co.uk/en/cworld
The Ironbridge Gorge Museums, Coalbrookdale, where you can learn about the history of industry and try some design and technology yourself. See
www.ironbridge.org.uk

Index